Herbert S. Zim and Lucretia Krantz

SEA STARS
AND THEIR KIN

illustrated by René Martin

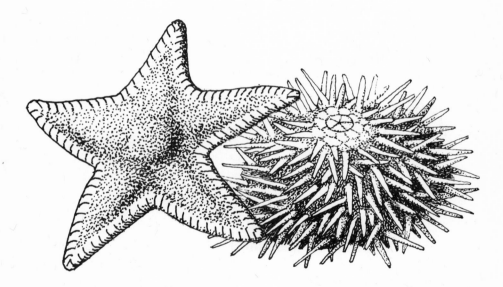

William Morrow and Company

New York   1976

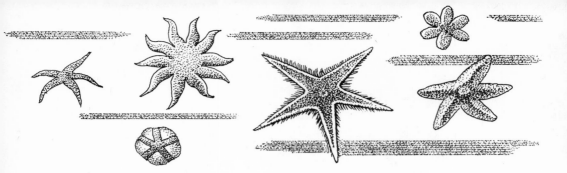

Printed in the United States of America.
1   2   3   4   5   79   78   77   76   75

Library of Congress Cataloging in Publication Data

Zim, Herbert Spencer
    Sea stars and their kin.

    SUMMARY: Introduces five kinds of starfish and describes their growth, reproduction, feeding, habitats, and relationship with human beings.
    1. Starfishes—Juvenile literature. [1. Starfishes. 2. Marine animals] I. Krantz, Lucretia, joint author, II. Martin, René, fl.
III. Title.
QL384.Z8Z55 1976   593'.93   75-17633
ISBN 0-688-22053-3
ISBN 0-688-32053-8 lib. bdg.

The authors join in thanking Lt. Col. Corinne E. Edwards USAF (Rtd.) of Coconut Grove, Florida, author of popular and technical articles on sea life, for reading and checking the manuscript. They are also indebted to Helen Lang of the National Marine Fisheries Service for assistance in locating resource materials.

The common, well-known starfish, or sea star, as it is more properly called, has long been a symbol of the sea. Its shape is the most distinct of any sea animal. These spiny, five-rayed creatures are one example of a very unusual group of marine animals with a life story different from that of anything else in the animal kingdom.

Sea stars and their relatives form a group, or phylum, called the echinoderms. The name means "spiny skinned," and most have just that kind of covering. A few land animals like porcupines and hedgehogs also have spiny skins. But these creatures are unrelated and differ from sea stars and their kin in many ways.

PORCUPINE

HEDGEHOG
rolled up

SINGLE AND JOINED CELLS

Some balls of cells
become radial animals
with a ring of tentacles around
their central mouth opening.

as seen from the outside

The open end
of a cup of cells
forms a mouth.

Joined cells
form a ball.

as seen in cross section

tentacles

The first animals, living at least a billion years ago, were single cells, each alone and independent. Later the cells joined together, often forming a ball. In this way they could aid one another. From these simple kinds of many-celled animals, two body plans developed. The first plan was circular. The animal ball became a hollow cup with arms or tentacles around the top. This radial body plan is still seen in sponge animals, corals, and jellyfish.

The second body plan is built around a tube with a front and back end. Parts of the body develop equally on both sides of the tube in a two-sided, or bilateral, way. Most of the animals you know follow that plan.

The tube may seem completely hidden, yet it remains the path by which foods come in and wastes go out. Organs inside the body, such as kidneys, lungs, testes, and ovaries, are usually paired. The head has paired eyes, ears, and nostrils. Paired arms and legs also appear as wings, flippers, or fins.

ANIMALS WITH A TUBELIKE BODY PLAN

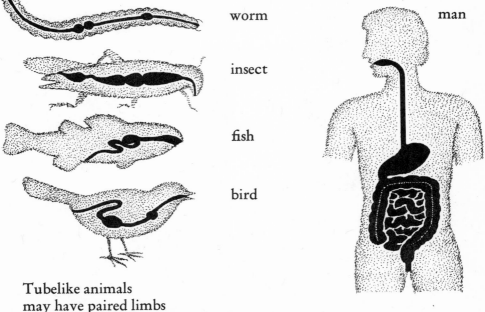

worm

insect

fish

bird

man

Tubelike animals
may have paired limbs
and other paired body parts.

Echinoderms look like examples of the radial plan, but instead they are the first animals to use the bilateral plan. When a sea-star egg hatches into a small larva, its body is balanced left and right. Like all echinoderms, it starts life on the bilateral plan, the plan that your body follows. Scarcely bigger than a pinhead, the larva is transparent and swims freely. But as the animal matures, it shifts quite rapidly to a body plan of five equal parts.

Living echinoderms include five closely related groups of animals, each with a scientific Latin name. Commonly they are known as sea stars, brittle stars, sea urchins, sea cucumbers, and sea lilies. All have several features in common not found in other animals.

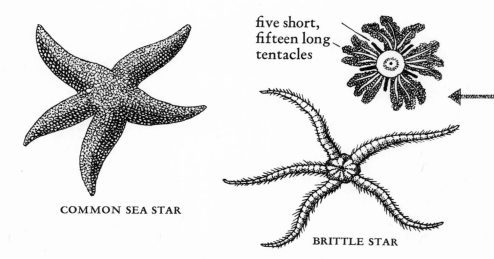

COMMON SEA STAR

five short, fifteen long tentacles

BRITTLE STAR

All echinoderms are sea dwellers. None live in fresh water — rivers or lakes — or on land. They have neither head nor tail, and they have no paired body parts. Some, however, have a front and back end. Their five-part radial bodies often have five rays, or arms. Some are oval or flattened in shape.

All echinoderms have seawater flowing through canals and tubes in their bodies. This arrangement forms an odd water-vascular system, which no other group of animals has. The animal moves by pumping water, under pressure, into many small tube feet, or podia. All echinoderms have plates of lime that form a kind of skeleton within their skin. The larger plates often have spines, which give the group its name.

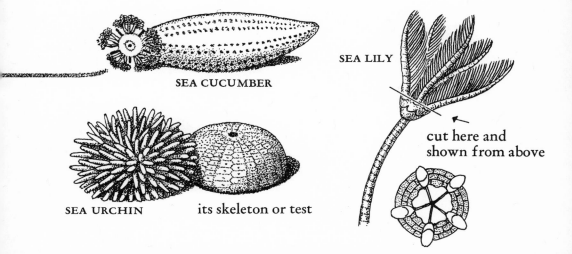

SEA CUCUMBER

SEA LILY

cut here and shown from above

SEA URCHIN

its skeleton or test

Crinoids, which include sea lilies and sea feathers, are the oldest and perhaps the strangest echinoderms. These animals grow on a stalk or rest on the bottom. Thus, their mouth opens above instead of below as is true of most other echinoderms. When the first crinoids were hauled to the surface, they looked so much like plants that they were named sea lilies. Other sea animals, like sea plumes and sea fans, have also been mistaken for plants.

CRINOIDS

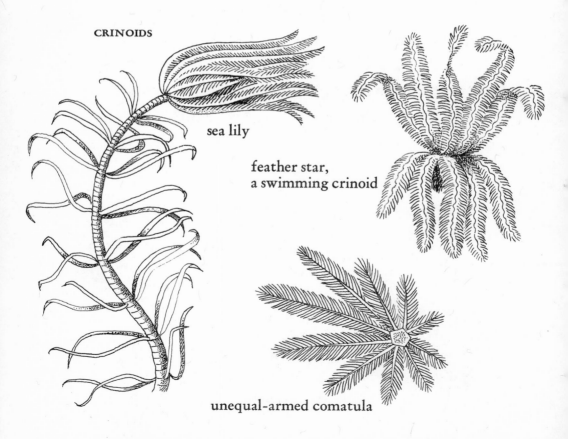

sea lily

feather star,
a swimming crinoid

unequal-armed comatula

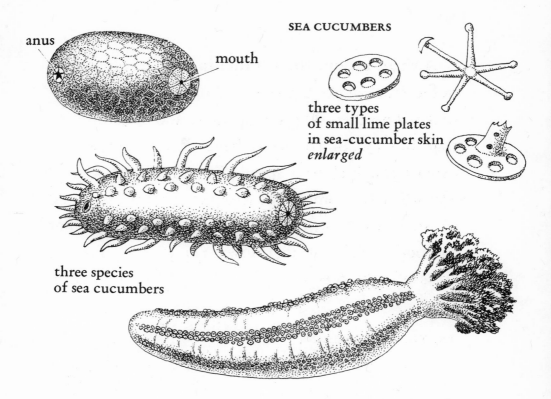

anus

mouth

three types
of small lime plates
in sea-cucumber skin
enlarged

three species
of sea cucumbers

Another group, the sea cucumbers, have very
few and very small plates of lime scattered in their
thick skin. These overstuffed, cucumberlike creatures, like other echinoderms, have five areas of
tube feet. Some of these feet, around the mouth,
have become tentacles. However, while their relatives live in an up-and-down position, sea cucumbers lie on one side.

A third group, the sea urchins, have spines that range from short bristles to stout spines and fine-toothed needles. The sand dollars and cake urchins that burrow in the sand have flatter bodies and usually much shorter spines. The urchin's body, an armored disc, sometimes irregular or oval, is called a test. In this test, the limy plates are so fused that the body itself cannot move. Yet it, too, has five areas of tube feet.

IRREGULAR SEA URCHINS

Atlantic sand-dollar test

One group of sea urchins has irregular tests, or shells, and short spines.

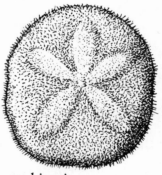

sea biscuit

test of notched sand dollar

club urchin

long-spined sea urchin

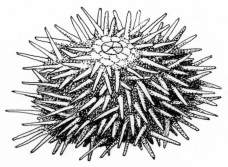

short-spined sea urchin

cidarid with fan-shaped spines

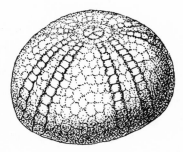

test of purple sea urchin

Regular sea urchins live
locked in a round or oval test,
a few of which reach
30 centimeters in diameter.
Their spines,
sometimes 25 centimeters long,
may be poisonous.

The creatures that used to be called starfish and now are known as sea stars are really two groups: the sea stars and the more delicate, lesser known brittle stars. Sea stars have a central body disc that blends into its radiating arms, or rays. The central disc of brittle stars is distinct and set off from its arms. The limy, spined plates of the sea star are imbedded in a tough skin. Brittle stars have even more of them, but both can move their arms freely.

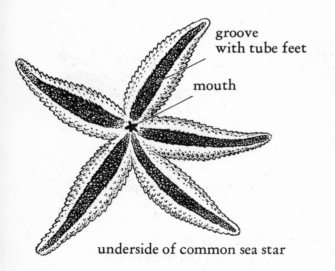

groove
with tube feet

mouth

underside of common sea star

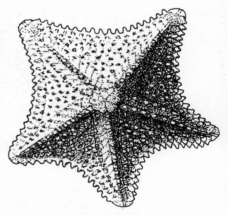

West Indian sea star

The skeleton of sea stars
is mainly fibers
in which many plates of lime
are embedded.
The plates have ridges, bumps, or spines.
Some sea stars also have tiny pincers
that can grasp and hold.

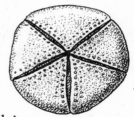

culcita,
a sea star without rays

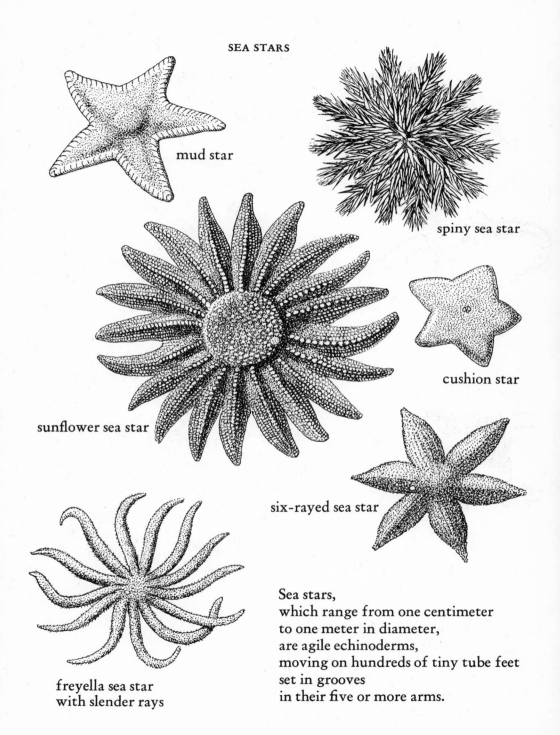

SEA STARS

mud star

spiny sea star

sunflower sea star

cushion star

six-rayed sea star

freyella sea star
with slender rays

Sea stars,
which range from one centimeter
to one meter in diameter,
are agile echinoderms,
moving on hundreds of tiny tube feet
set in grooves
in their five or more arms.

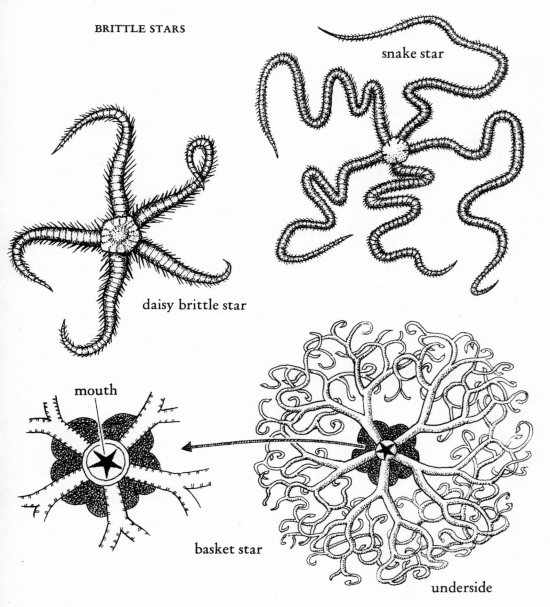

snake star

daisy brittle star

mouth

basket star

underside

Brittle stars,
though they look like sea stars,
are quite different.
They lack grooves on their arms
and have few tube feet,
yet they move around vigorously,
using extended arms to pull and row.

About 2,000 kinds of starfish and 1,600 brittle stars are known. In addition, there are some 750 kinds of sea urchins, 600 sea lilies, and 500 sea cucumbers. Thus, almost 6,000 kinds, or species, of marine animals form the phylum of echinoderms. But some 6,000 species makes only a small phylum. The backboned animals, from fish up to man, include 45,000 different kinds. Insects total nearly a million species.

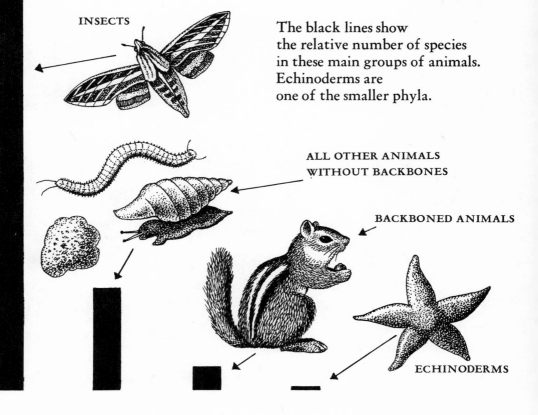

INSECTS

The black lines show
the relative number of species
in these main groups of animals.
Echinoderms are
one of the smaller phyla.

ALL OTHER ANIMALS
WITHOUT BACKBONES

BACKBONED ANIMALS

ECHINODERMS

Sea stars and their kin have been around for five hundred million years or more. In fact, they were more common in the past than they are today. Three groups, well known as fossils, have died out and are now extinct. No living member of these groups has ever been seen. Some 20,000 kinds of fossil echinoderms have been found and named. These fossils show only a few differences between the ancient species and those living today.

FOSSIL ECHINODERMS

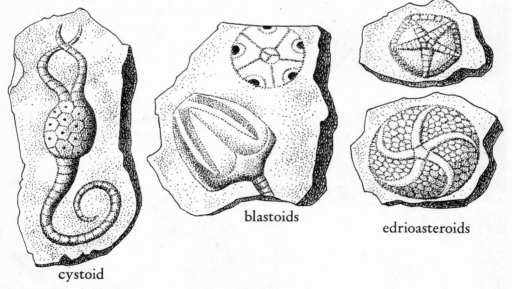

blastoids

edrioasteroids

cystoid

More echinoderms and more kinds of echinoderms lived millions of years ago than are living today. These are examples of three important groups that are now extinct.

Sea stars and other echinoderms have found ways to live on nearly every part of the ocean bottom. They have been collected from the cold waters of the Arctic and Antarctic. Special submarines that explore the deepest parts of the ocean have taken photographs of echinoderms there. Visitors to tropical beaches and coral reefs find many beautiful and unusual kinds. Echinoderms are most common, in numbers and in species, in the warm parts of the Pacific Ocean. They are quite plentiful in the Caribbean too. At one time many thousands were collected each year on the Florida Keys. Most were cleaned and sold in local stores.

Over millions of years, echinoderms have settled down in parts of the ocean bottom best suited for them. Most avoided muddy bottoms, but one starfish, the mud star, is so named because it prefers mud. Deep-sea urchins and heart urchins may live on mud bottoms also. However, muddy or polluted water, shifting sands, and silting may kill echinoderms.

Many of these animals prefer rocky places. Some sea urchins use their stout spines to burrow into the soft coral rock, making a cup into which the urchin fits. There it remains all its life. Sea urchins have been known to cut and scrape their way into concrete.

Sea stars and their kin are found singly or in small groups. However, at some times and in some places, they come together in large numbers. Thousands of globular sea urchins cover nearly all the bottom of some tropical bays. Hundreds of sea stars, instead of the normal ten or twenty, gather where the water temperature is better, or where there is more food. Some move or migrate to areas where they lay eggs, or spawn. Then they travel on to less crowded parts of the ocean.

Echinoderms are not great travelers. Their larvae can swim well and are carried long distances by ocean currents. The feather star, a crinoid, can also swim a bit. So can some of the brittle stars, which use two arms on either side as oars. Sea cucumbers, sea urchins, brittle stars, and sea stars move around, but slowly. Most sea lilies anchor themselves to rocky bottoms.

HOW ECHINODERMS MOVE

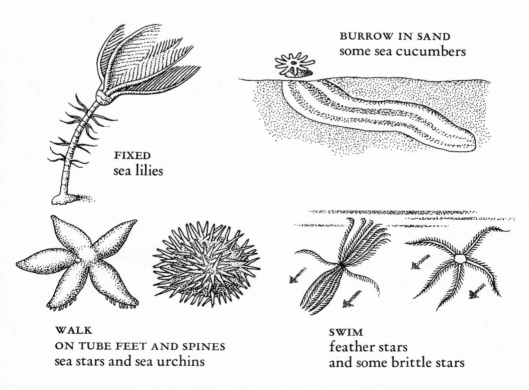

BURROW IN SAND
some sea cucumbers

FIXED
sea lilies

WALK
ON TUBE FEET AND SPINES
sea stars and sea urchins

SWIM
feather stars
and some brittle stars

To move, most echinoderms also use their flexible tube feet, which are the ends of the water-vascular system. Muscles squeeze the swollen tops of the tube feet, putting the water under pressure and pushing the tube feet out. In this way the animal controls the tube feet and their movement. Suckers at the end of the tube feet take hold of the sand or shell or rock. The echinoderm pulls itself forward. Then the animal relaxes some of its tube feet and moves them up to take a new grip.

Thus, sea stars move forward on hundreds of tube feet set in a groove that goes the length of each arm, or ray. But the speed is slow. Some move two to five centimeters a minute or a bit faster, although one has been clocked doing two meters per minute, nearly a hundred times the average speed.

Brittle stars lack grooves in their rays and suckers on their tube feet. But they use them to move, climb, and burrow anyhow. Using their arms to push and pull, these most active echinoderms move as fast as 1.8 meters per minute.

Sea cucumbers jerk along by waves of muscles moving through their bodies. These muscle waves start at the rear and move the animal forward. In this way a sea cucumber will progress one meter in about fifteen minutes. Some sea cucumbers have rows of tube feet, and some use their tentacles to help them along.

A body wave starting at the rear
sends the sea cucumber forward slowly.

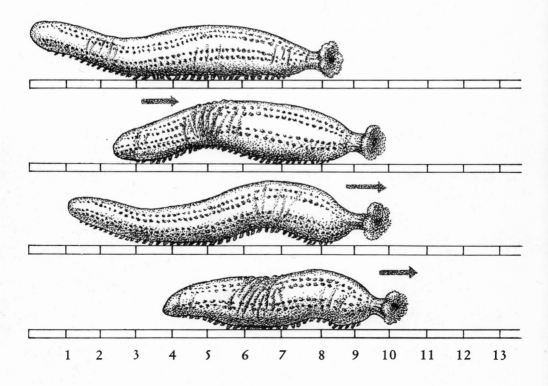

1   2   3   4   5   6   7   8   9   10   11   12   13

Most sea urchins are much faster. They move about with their short tube feet and their spines. When they climb on rock, the tube feet are most helpful. A sea urchin, using only its tube feet, moves about one centimeter a minute. But using its spines, it can move up to three hundred times as fast.

Sea stars and their kin respond to the ocean and to its changes. Those kinds that live close to the shore may be exposed to the air when the tide is low. As long as they remain moist and shaded, they can stand exposure to the air for hours — even for a day. But none of these animals can survive when it gets completely dry.

high-water line

low-water line

A special
deep-sea-exploration
submarine
spots and photographs
echinoderms
and other sea life
in waters that are
over a half mile deep.

Some echinoderms live in deep water that remains only a few degrees above freezing. Some live
in shallow water, where the temperature changes
daily and with the seasons. Cells in the skins of
starfish and other echinoderms detect these temperature changes. Then the animals usually move
toward water with a temperature that is better for
them.

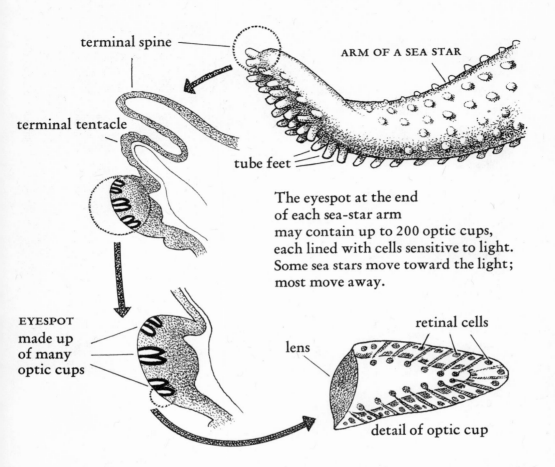

terminal spine

ARM OF A SEA STAR

terminal tentacle

tube feet

The eyespot at the end
of each sea-star arm
may contain up to 200 optic cups,
each lined with cells sensitive to light.
Some sea stars move toward the light;
most move away.

EYESPOT
made up
of many
optic cups

retinal cells

lens

detail of optic cup

Sea stars also respond to light. At the tip of each
ray is a tiny eyespot. This spot has cup-shaped
organs, lined with cells that are sensitive to light.
When daylight is too bright, many echinoderms
move toward more shaded places.

These animals detect the chemicals in seawater and other materials. Sea stars can locate and move toward one bit of oyster meat in a large aquarium tank. When water becomes muddy, they usually move away. If floods dilute the salt water near the shore, echinoderms head toward saltier water.

Sea urchins and sea stars respond to gravity as well. They know when they have been turned upside down by a child or a fish. By the use of tube feet or spines, the animal will turn over to its normal mouth-down position. The echinoderm's sense of touch also helps it keep its balance.

SEA STAR TURNING OVER

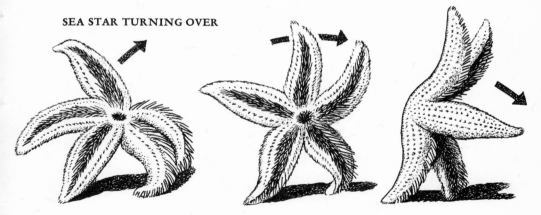

Grasping the sea floor
with its tube feet,
the sea star begins to raise
two or three arms vertically.
Then, moving one or more arms forward,
displacing the center of gravity,
it turns over.

Overall, however, sea urchins, sea cucumbers, and sea stars are not very sensitive animals. Their reactions are mainly automatic. And what senses they have are of limited use, because echinoderms do not have a brain. A ring of nerve cells collects the input of information. It signals the animal to change its position or to take some other kind of action.

SEA URCHIN'S NERVE RING

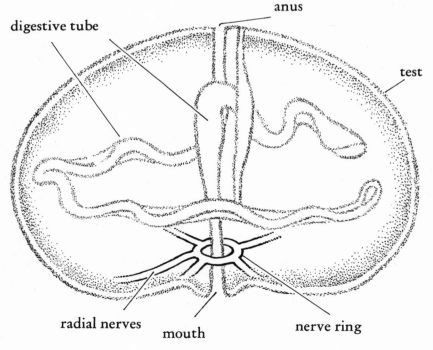

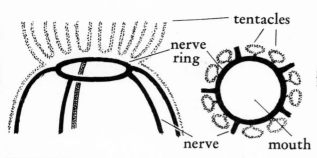

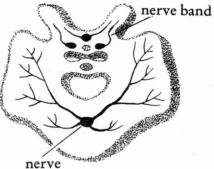

**NERVE RING
AROUND MOUTH OF SEA CUCUMBER**

**NERVE BAND AND NERVES
IN ARM OF CRINOID**

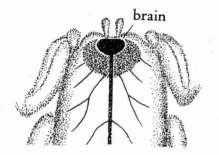

With only the shadow of a brain
echinoderms get sensations
of light, heat, and gravity,
but they react automatically.
When nerves join to make a simple brain,
better reactions are possible.

Some echinoderms have three nerve rings instead of one. One ring may follow the water-vascular system, and one may branch out into arms, or rays. Some have more nerves around the mouth. Experts think that the nerve rings are the beginnings of a brain, but they are not very much of a beginning.

Echinoderms are all well-protected animals, shielded from enemies by sharp spines, armored plates, or tough skin. Some hide; some burrow; a few are poisonous. Protection helps them survive. In addition, they persist and hold their place in the ocean because most have large numbers of young. Reproduction protects the group of animals and helps them to survive just as spines and armor protect each individual echinoderm.

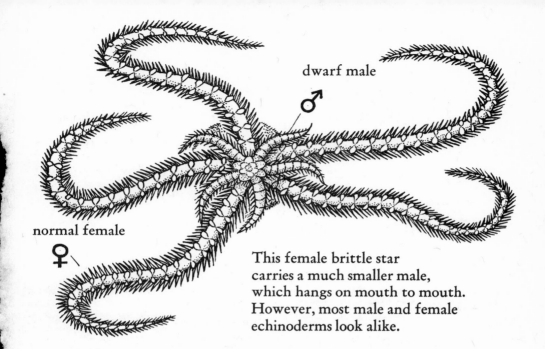

dwarf male

♂

normal female

♀

This female brittle star carries a much smaller male, which hangs on mouth to mouth. However, most male and female echinoderms look alike.

Reproduction of sea stars and their kin usually requires a male and a female, but not always. How can you tell the sexes apart? You usually cannot without careful study, but the female can best be spotted when she is full of eggs. A few kinds show other differences. The female of one sea star, in the warm parts of the Pacific, is slightly larger than the male. In one unusual group of brittle stars, the dwarf males cling to the much larger females.

Male echinoderms produce sperm, and females make eggs. When both are ripe, they are released into the sea. Large females may release 200 million eggs or so when they spawn. The males release clouds of sperm first or at about the same time. Many thousands of eggs are fertilized.

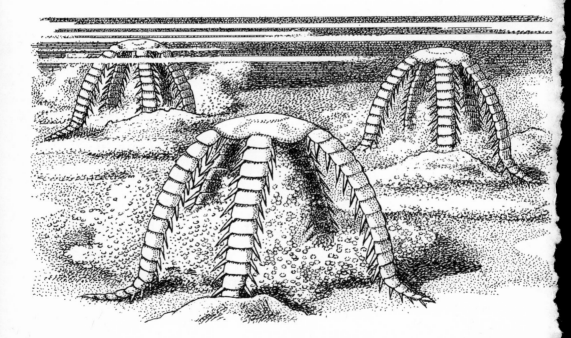

When spawning, usually in spring and summer, some brittle stars raise their central disc. Sperm and eggs are released into the water.

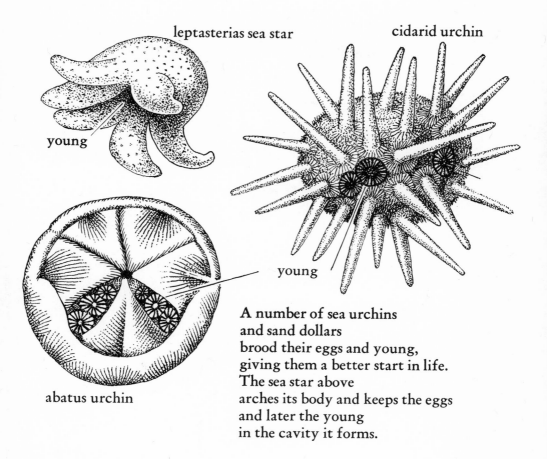

leptasterias sea star

cidarid urchin

young

young

abatus urchin

A number of sea urchins
and sand dollars
brood their eggs and young,
giving them a better start in life.
The sea star above
arches its body and keeps the eggs
and later the young
in the cavity it forms.

Some sea urchins and sea stars that live in very
cold water protect their eggs by brooding them in
pouches near their mouth. These females produce
only one or two hundred eggs at a time instead of
millions.

The gonads, organs that produce the sperm or the eggs, are in different parts of the body in different kinds of echinoderms. Sea stars have, in each arm, two gonads that look like very small bunches of grapes. During the spawning season, these bunches enlarge and grow till they nearly fill the entire arm. One sea cucumber has gonads that look like a miniature mop inside the mouth. Crinoids have, in the middle of their arms, small groups of

GONADS

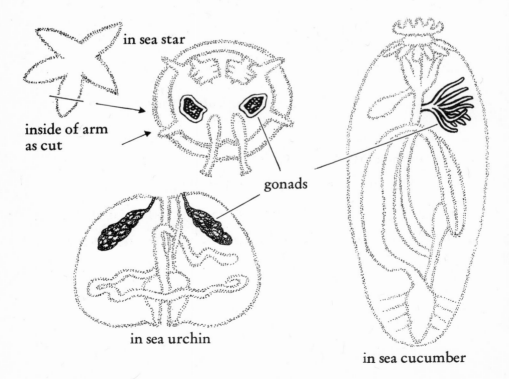

in sea star

inside of arm as cut

gonads

in sea urchin

in sea cucumber

sex cells that may produce either sperm or eggs.

Some kinds of sea stars, brittle stars, and sea cucumbers have only a single gonad. This gonad may make sperm and eggs at the same time. Or it may alternate, first making sperm, then eggs. In an even odder arrangement, some sea cucumbers start out as females. After the gonad has produced eggs, it goes to pieces. Then a new male gonad, which makes sperm, forms.

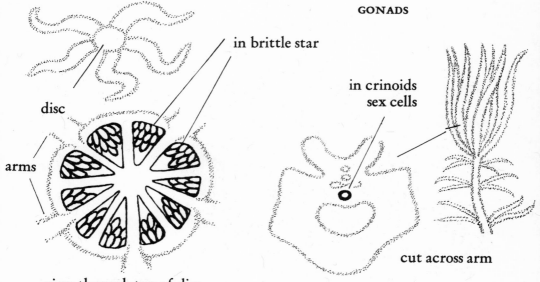

GONADS

in brittle star

in crinoids
sex cells

disc

arms

view through top of disc

cut across arm

Most echinoderms are either male or female,
but in some species
the individual can make both eggs and sperm.
The eggs are usually fertilized
as they float in the sea.

The spawning of sea stars and other echinoderms usually takes place in spring, but some kinds spawn more than once a year. Sometimes the period of spawning is set precisely. One crinoid (*Comanthus*) spawns once a year, on about the same day during the last half of October. The moon is always either at the first or last quarter. On the proper day this simple animal will spawn in the late afternoon.

Comanthus

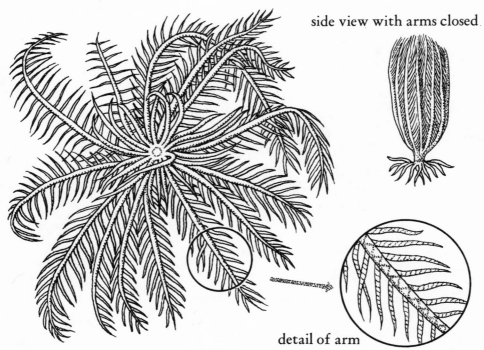

side view with arms closed

detail of arm

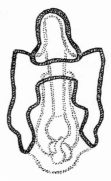

very young larva
of sea urchin

young larva
of sea star

older larva
of sea star

Within a few days after spawning, the fertilized
eggs have grown into tiny, swimming larvae. Larvae feed on plankton, microscopic plants and
animals. They change as they grow. This growth
may be as short as a week or two or as long as three
months. It is a dangerous time. Many of the unpro-
tected larvae die or are eaten. At the right time, the
larvae change rapidly and become adults. For sea
urchins and sea stars, this process happens in a few
hours. A heavy shell develops. The animal sinks to
the bottom, where it soon feeds, grows, and acts
like other adults.

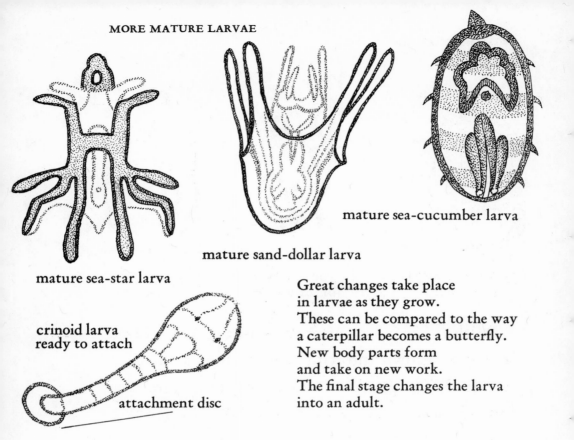

mature sea-cucumber larva

mature sand-dollar larva

mature sea-star larva

crinoid larva
ready to attach

attachment disc

Great changes take place
in larvae as they grow.
These can be compared to the way
a caterpillar becomes a butterfly.
New body parts form
and take on new work.
The final stage changes the larva
into an adult.

The growth of the larva is not a simple matter. It changes from a clump of cells to a ball; then parts for feeding and movement develop. Many larvae undergo major changes in form as they grow. Some remain floating or free swimming; others move toward the bottom. All go there just before they change into their adult form.

The great dangers that larvae face are avoided by the cold-water echinoderms that brood their eggs. These eggs do not become free-swimming larvae. They hatch as very small adults, which live on their own. Their growth is mainly an increase in size.

Sea stars and sea urchins have grown enough to spawn after a year or so. Brittle stars seem to take a year longer, and sea cucumbers may not spawn till their third or fourth year. Less is known about how long echinoderms live — probably three to ten years under good conditions.

AGE AT WHICH SOME ECHINODERMS MATURE AND SPAWN

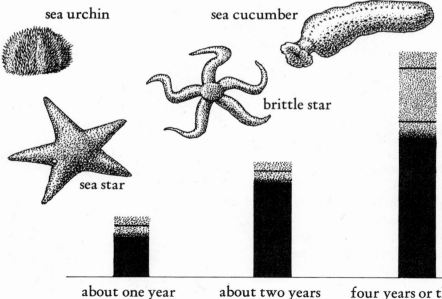

sea urchin sea cucumber

brittle star

sea star

about one year   about two years   four years or three years

As they mature, sea stars, brittle stars, and sea cucumbers also reproduce without the other sex. This process is called asexual reproduction. The center disc of a starfish may divide into halves. Each half grows the missing parts and becomes a new sea star. The common starfish *Linckia* may cast off one or more of its arms. Then each arm forms a new disc, and the new disc forms new arms.

THE NATURAL PROCESS OF ASEXUAL REPRODUCTION

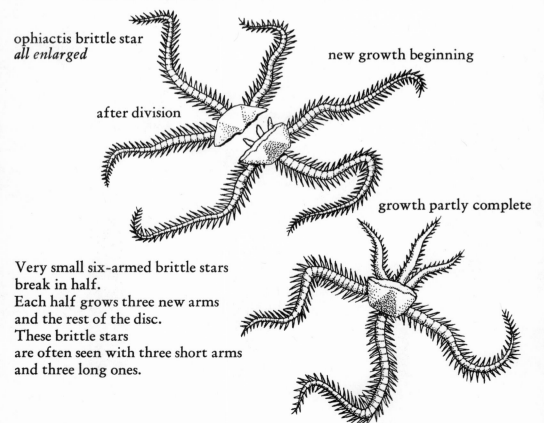

ophiactis brittle star
all enlarged

new growth beginning

after division

growth partly complete

Very small six-armed brittle stars
break in half.
Each half grows three new arms
and the rest of the disc.
These brittle stars
are often seen with three short arms
and three long ones.

Sea stars and their kin also have a unique process of growth and repair. All living things can, to a degree, repair injuries. But what your body can do for a cut or a scratch, a sea star can do for an entire arm. This major repair, or replacement, is called regeneration. Echinoderms are famous for this process, but regeneration varies from one class of echinoderms to another.

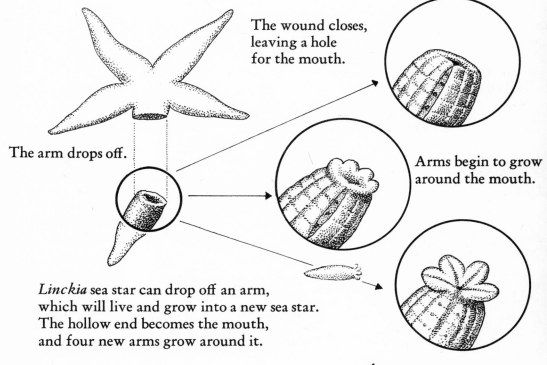

The wound closes, leaving a hole for the mouth.

The arm drops off.

Arms begin to grow around the mouth.

Linckia sea star can drop off an arm, which will live and grow into a new sea star. The hollow end becomes the mouth, and four new arms grow around it.

Arms grow more in the comet stage.

Regeneration of body parts may take place in such a way that it becomes reproduction. When a sea star is cut in half, each half will regenerate into a new sea star. If cut in thirds, three new sea stars result. If cut into five parts, each consisting of one arm and a piece of the central disc, five new sea stars will form. A year or more is needed to grow the remaining portion of the disc and the four new arms.

REGENERATION AS ASEXUAL REPRODUCTION

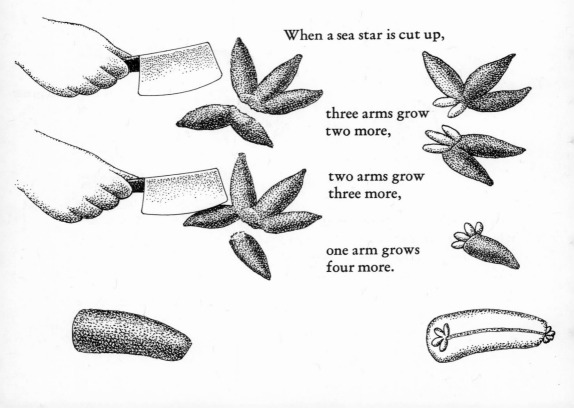

When a sea star is cut up,

three arms grow
two more,

two arms grow
three more,

one arm grows
four more.

A special boat for mopping oyster beds
brings the sea stars ashore.

Because of their ability to regenerate, sea stars
once caused a serious problem in the New England
oyster beds. Both the sea stars and the fishermen
want the oysters, and the sea stars often get them
first. So when oystermen brought sea stars to the
surface with their oysters, they killed them by
chopping the sea star in half. Thousands upon
thousands of sea stars were chopped and thrown
overboard. Each year more and more starfish
seemed to appear in the oyster beds. Slowly the
oyster fishermen became aware of what they were
doing. Then they dumped the sea stars ashore,
where the dry air soon killed them.

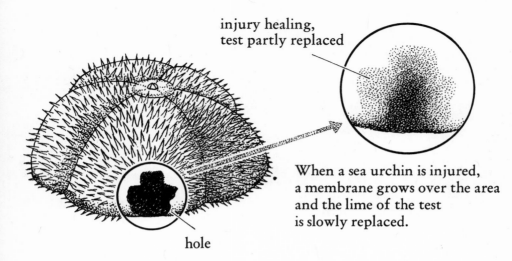

injury healing,
test partly replaced

When a sea urchin is injured,
a membrane grows over the area
and the lime of the test
is slowly replaced.

hole

A brittle star can regenerate its arms but not its disc. So most regeneration is only for repair, since the entire disc is usually needed. Only a small group of brittle stars can reproduce by regeneration.

Regeneration is also limited for sea urchins, sand dollars, heart urchins, and crinoids. These animals make repairs, but they do not reproduce by regeneration. The sea cucumber can, but only to a small degree. If one is cut in half, the front end will regenerate. Sea cucumbers also use regeneration in a very different and more complex way.

Inside the food tube of the sea cucumber is a mass of tiny sticky tubes, or tubules. They are used for protection. When a sea cucumber is attacked, it expels these sticky parts through its anus. The attacker may become entangled in the sticky mass. The sea cucumber, free from danger, then regenerates a whole new set of tubules.

SEA-CUCUMBER TUBULES ENTANGLING A FISH

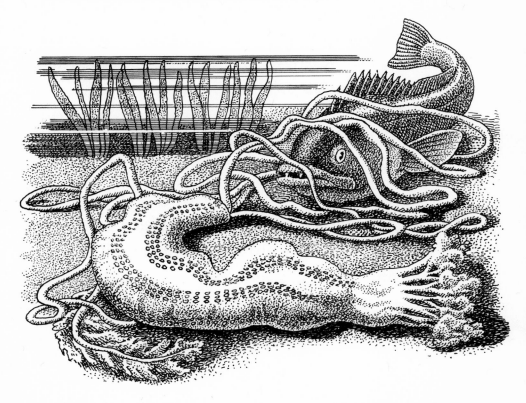

SEA CUCUMBERS EXPELLING THEIR INTERNAL ORGANS

A sea cucumber can also expel most of its internal organs through a split in the walls of its skin or its anus. It throws out its digestive tract, gonads, and nearly everything else. Just the thick skin of the animal is left to heal and regenerate.

Why sea cucumbers take this heroic step is not clear. They may be trying to escape an enemy. Yet the process also happens in dirty water or crowded conditions without a threat of danger. At any rate, the animal's need for food and oxygen is greatly cut down. It can stay alive as it quite rapidly regenerates all the lost organs and resumes its old way of life.

Your body is well organized into a number of interlocking systems. One of them takes food and changes it for the body's use. Another carries digested food and oxygen to all the cells of your body. Still another helps remove waste.

Sea stars and their kin do not have all your body systems, and you do not have all of theirs. The water-vascular system is an example. Water enters through a button-shaped opening. From this opening a canal leads to a ring. Smaller canals branch from the ring. Each ends in a tube foot, or podia.

WATER SYSTEM OF A SEA STAR

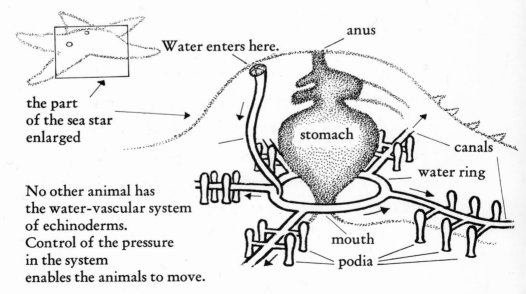

Water enters here.

anus

the part
of the sea star
enlarged

stomach

canals

water ring

No other animal has
the water-vascular system
of echinoderms.
Control of the pressure
in the system
enables the animals to move.

mouth

podia

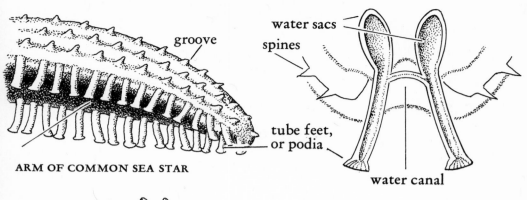

groove

water sacs

spines

tube feet,
or podia

water canal

ARM OF COMMON SEA STAR

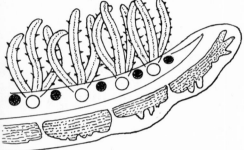

PODIA OF A CRINOID

Water-vascular systems
end in the tube feet, or podia.
These are moved by pressure changes
controlled by the water sacs,
which can also create suction
to give the podia a tight grip.

This system, always full of seawater, follows a different plan in each kind of echinoderm. Tubes go to the arms of sea stars or around the tests of sea urchins. Sea cucumbers do not use seawater entirely but also fluids from their stomach. Their system extends into their tentacles as well.

All these animals have a digestive tube. Usually it has two ends, sometimes only one. When the tube has two ends, food comes in at the mouth, is digested, and waste passes out through the anus. When the tube has only one end, the hairlike cells that move the food in set up reverse currents that carry the wastes out through the mouth.

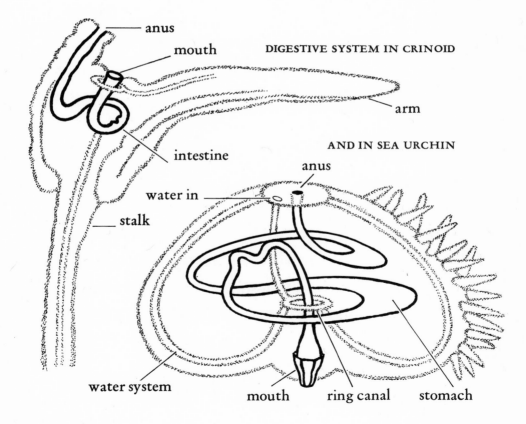

DIGESTIVE SYSTEM IN CRINOID

AND IN SEA URCHIN

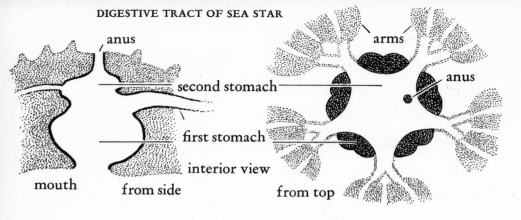

anus

arms

second stomach

anus

first stomach

interior view

mouth

from side

from top

Above the mouth of a sea star
a first stomach leads into a second.
This one has ducts going into each arm.
Higher are the intestine and anus.

Most sea stars and their kin have a separate stomach and intestine. The stomach often has two chambers. Instead of bringing food into the stomach, however, some sea stars send the stomach out to the food. After a sea star gets a clam or an oyster open, its stomach is pushed out through its mouth and in between the open shells. The delicate stomach can move through a crack less than one millimeter wide. Inside the shell its juices digest the soft parts of the clam or oyster. The digested food flows through the stomach back into the starfish. Other sea stars feed in more usual ways.

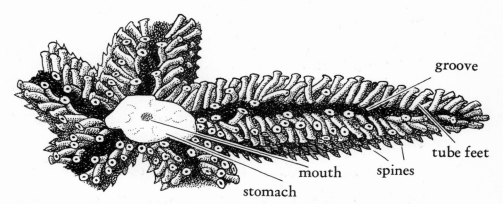

groove

tube feet

spines

mouth

stomach

UNDERSIDE OF A SEA STAR
showing mouth from which stomach has emerged

Some sea stars can push their delicate stomachs out
through their mouth and against the food they wish to eat.
This might be living coral or a living clam within its shell.
Only the digested food passes back into the sea star.

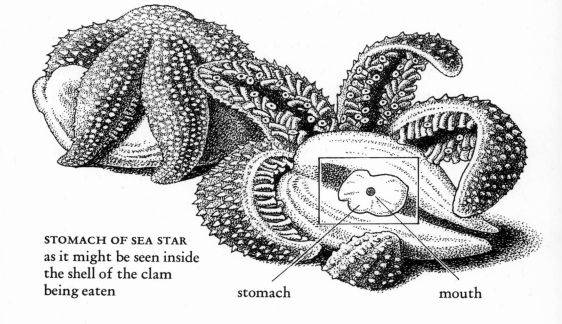

STOMACH OF SEA STAR
as it might be seen inside
the shell of the clam
being eaten

stomach

mouth

Sea stars and their kin do not really have a heart, but they do have some blood cells that contain the same red chemical as in your blood. The echinoderm's blood moves around in open spaces instead of through tubes as in your body. Some echinoderms do have short blood vessels going into the arms or through the body. These do not form a closed system, however, the way your veins and arteries do.

The vessels, or sinuses, often follow those of the water-vascular system and also lie close to the stomach and intestines. Many small branches connect to these organs and help move digested food to all parts inside the echinoderm.

While there is no heart to pump the fluid along, there seems to be some kind of beating, or contraction, which keeps the fluid in motion. This hemal system, as it is called, is most highly developed in sea cucumbers, where it also runs close to the special organs that help take oxygen from seawater.

Your blood system carries oxygen as well as digested food. The echinoderm's system carries mainly food. Oxygen is dissolved in the water that enters through small, bulbous organs. Most of the cells of an echinoderm are in contact with this water. From it they take the oxygen they need.

DIAGRAM OF BLOOD SYSTEMS

OF A BRITTLE STAR   OF A CRINOID

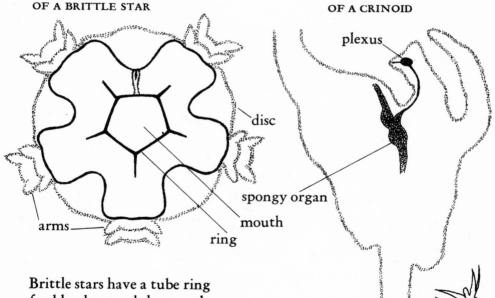

plexus

disc

spongy organ

arms

mouth

ring

blood cell
of a crinoid

Brittle stars have a tube ring for blood around the mouth which connects to a larger ring around the edge of the disc. Branches go into the arms. Crinoids have a spongy organ with blood cells and a few vessels connecting to it.

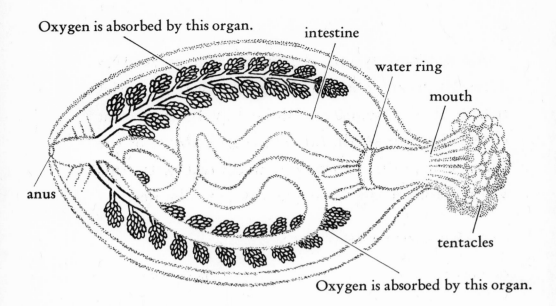

Oxygen is absorbed by this organ.

intestine

water ring

mouth

anus

tentacles

Oxygen is absorbed by this organ.

OXYGEN SYSTEM OF A SEA CUCUMBER

Some sea cucumbers get oxygen in an unusual way. They have thin branched sacs that connect with the hind end of their digestive tube. Muscles on these sacs squeeze them, and so pump water in and out. This water supplies dissolved oxygen to the animal. Most animals take in oxygen through the front end of their tubes. These sea cucumbers are the only animals in the world that take it in from the rear.

All echinoderms need food, and all start life with a bit of food stored in the egg. This supply keeps the unborn animal alive until it hatches. Then the free-swimming larvae trap tiny plants and animals for food. As they move around, they have a better chance to feed.

FOOD AND EARLY GROWTH OF ECHINODERMS

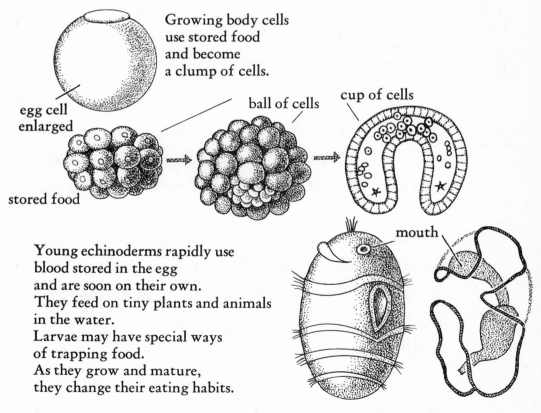

Growing body cells use stored food and become a clump of cells.

egg cell enlarged

stored food

ball of cells

cup of cells

mouth

Young echinoderms rapidly use blood stored in the egg and are soon on their own. They feed on tiny plants and animals in the water. Larvae may have special ways of trapping food. As they grow and mature, they change their eating habits.

two kinds of larvae

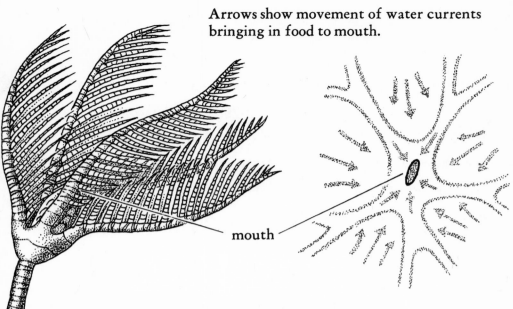

Arrows show movement of water currents bringing in food to mouth.

mouth

LOCATION AND DETAIL OF MOUTH OF SEA LILY

When larvae change into adults they change their way of feeding again. Crinoids and basket stars use their five or more arms, which are divided and divided again until they form a broad mesh, or network. The smallest parts are covered with hairlike, sticky cells. Waves and currents in the water wash bits of seaweed, fish eggs, larvae, and debris against these sticky cells. Thus, food is caught and passed along to the mouth.

Sea cucumbers feed more actively but in about the same way. They sweep their mouth tentacles over the bottom or wave them in the water. The sticky surface traps larvae, small plants, and animals. Every now and then the tentacles are pulled in. As the tentacles push out again, the food is wiped off within the mouth.

Some sea cucumbers that live buried on the bottom feed directly on sand and mud. As they suck this mud and water through their body, bits of food and even small animals come in with it. The sea cucumbers feed on these particles. Such animals are called filter feeders. They pick up a great deal of sand or mud and separate their food from it.

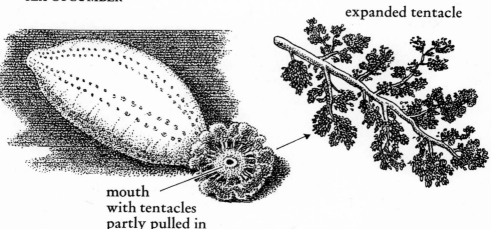

SEA CUCUMBER

expanded tentacle

mouth
with tentacles
partly pulled in

Sea stars, sea urchins, and brittle stars do move around in search of food. They feed on oysters, clams, mussels, barnacles, worms, sea plants, and sometimes on other echinoderms. They also feed on any dead animals they find. Some starfish prefer one special kind of animal food, such as sponges, sea anemones, oysters, or coral animals. Sea urchins prefer plant food.

eaten coral

THE CROWN-OF-THORNS SEA STAR
FEEDING ON CORAL

Finding a clam or oyster is something of a task, since sea stars cannot "see." But once a clam is found, how does the starfish get it open? The sea star moves over the closed clam and surrounds it with its arms. The tube feet make contact with both shells and set up a suction, or pull, against them. This pull may be between one and five thousand grams.

The clam's large muscles hold its shells together. The sea star, with its slow, steady pull, works against them. In an hour or two the clamshell slowly opens.

However, the sea star can work its stomach into even tiny cracks, such as those between the shell's irregular edges. So the sea star's stomach chemicals may be what affect the clam's muscles rather than the pull on them. Perhaps both these actions take place together. At any rate, the clamshell opens and the sea star feeds on the living animal. During this kind of feeding no waste products are taken in or excreted.

Several types of tiny pincers are found
on the skins of sea stars and sea urchins.
Some are poisonous.
They protect the animal and help it get its food.

 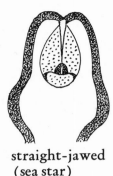 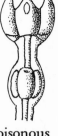 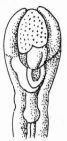

cross-jawed   straight-jawed   poisonous   heavy-jawed
(sea star)   (sea star)   (sea urchin)   (sea urchin)

Sea urchins and sea stars have specialized organs like tiny pincers near their spines. They use these to capture food, to hold it, and move it to the mouth. The pincers are also used for protection; some have poison glands. The sea urchin uses its spines to move food around also. Sea urchins have a special set of five "teeth" in a structure known as Aristotle's lantern. These teeth are used to grind and chew food.

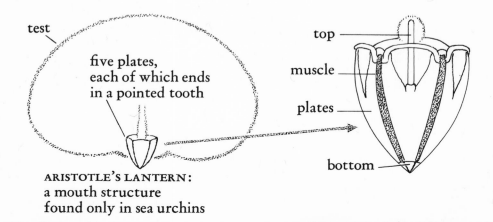

test

five plates,
each of which ends
in a pointed tooth

top

muscle

plates

bottom

ARISTOTLE'S LANTERN:
a mouth structure
found only in sea urchins

Some sea animals feed on sea urchins, sea stars, and their well-protected kin. These echinoderms are more vulnerable from below. Puffers and other coral-reef fish push or squirt a jet of water to turn a sea urchin or sea star over. Then they attack the less protected underside with their heavy teeth, tearing the animal open and feeding on the soft inner parts. Gulls take sea urchins ashore, when they can seize them at low tide, and feed on them in the same way. Sea otters and walruses also eat echinoderms. So do a few of the very large marine snails.

The main enemy of echinoderms seems to be the one that endangers all of nature — man. Man is dangerous to echinoderms when he pollutes shallow waters where many live. He is more dangerous when he upsets the marine environment.

Some echinoderms are used as human food. In Europe and other places people consider them a delicacy. Local people gather sea cucumbers along warm Pacific shores. They split them open, boil them, and dry them. The tough animal, called trepang, is later soaked and boiled to make thick, tasty soups. People also cut open sea urchins and eat the tasty eggs inside. Sea urchins and other echinoderms make chemicals that may be used in medicine. Experiments with them are under way.

Sea-urchin spines may injure swimmers in tropical waters. Sometimes the thin spines of the urchin *Diadema* pierce the skin and break off. They are very difficult to remove. But the lime that makes the spines usually dissolves in the skin. In a week or so, no trace of the spine remains.

Some sea-urchin spines do contain a poison. When a large amount of it enters a person's skin, the poison causes the nearby muscles to become paralyzed. Swimmers and scuba divers learn to be careful when long-spined sea urchins are around. Some sea cucumbers are reported to be poisonous too, at least to small fish.

Some echinoderms do live closely and on good terms with other sea animals. The pearl fish, a thin creature about five inches long, lives inside the sea cucumber. It goes out at night to search for food. With daylight, it forces itself back into the food tube of the sea cucumber. The pearl fish does not harm the sea cucumber, but it does not seem to help it either.

The pearl fish
spends its days
within the digestive tube
of a sea cucumber.
At night it leaves
to find food,
returning to its shelter
at dawn.

In the warm, shallow waters of the Indian and Pacific Oceans, seven kinds of small shrimp live closely with echinoderms, especially with some sea urchins and sea stars. They cling to the spines of the host, where their color and long, narrow form make them hard to find. Other shrimp of the same group lead more normal, independent lives. Some mollusks also live attached to echinoderms.

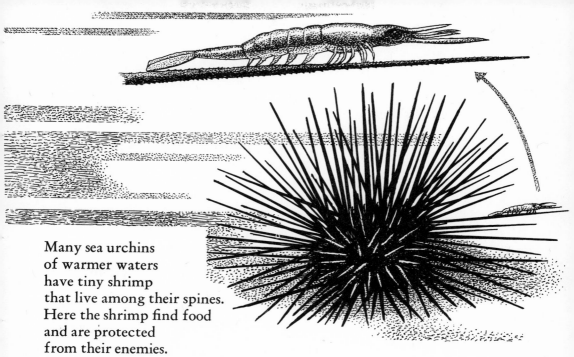

Many sea urchins
of warmer waters
have tiny shrimp
that live among their spines.
Here the shrimp find food
and are protected
from their enemies.

Echinoderms have made a place for themselves in the sea, where they survive. Well-protected and often hidden, they have remained unchanged through millions of years. They live their quiet lives in odd and interesting ways that show how complex a life-style can be. The whole group is one small and unusual part of the web of life that makes the sea so important.